Better Than God

Peter Porter ⋯ ⋯ ⋯ in Britain fifty yea⋯ ⋯ ⋯ ⋯ has lived here ever si⋯ ⋯. Since 1974 he has visited his native Australia often and considers himself part of the present-day poetical worlds of both nations. Since 1968 he has been a freelance literary journalist and reviewer. He has published seventeen books of poems, plus four further volumes with the Australian painter Arthur Boyd. He has been married twice and has, with his second wife, nine grandchildren.

Better Than God

Peter Porter

PICADOR

First published 2009 by Picador
an imprint of Pan Macmillan Ltd
Pan Macmillan, 20 New Wharf Road, London N1 9RR
Basingstoke and Oxford
Associated companies throughout the world
www.panmacmillan.com

ISBN 978-0-330-46067-5

9 8 7 6 5 4 3 2 1

A CIP catalogue record for this book is available from
the British Library.

Printed and bound in the UK by
CPI Mackays, Chatham ME5 8TD

Contents

Acknowledgements

Thanks are due to the editors and compilers of the following magazines, newspapers and periodicals in which some of these poems appeared: *The Age*, *Ambit*, *Australian Book Review*, *Australian Literary Review*, *Chimera*, *Fiddlehead*, *Lanterns*, *Meanjin*, *Poetry Review*, *Roundyhouse*, the *Spectator*, *Staple*, the *Times Literary Supplement*, *Warwick Review*. The following poems were included in *Eighteen Poems*, published by Shoestring Press, in 2006 – 'Because We Can', 'Glumdalclitch's Cleavage', 'Henry James and Constipation', 'How the Eureka Stockade Led to Boggo Road Gaol', 'In Bed with Oblomov', 'Leafing Through the Latin Dictionary', 'Money and Stravinsky', 'Opus 77', 'Ranunculus Which My Father Called a Poppy', 'Strontium to Mendeleyev', 'To Murder Sleep', 'Under the Rupe Tarpeia'. 'River Quatrains' was included in *Rivers*, published by Fremantle Arts Press in 2002. 'The Hungarian Producer Goes to Lunch' appeared in *Return to Kerguelen* (Vagabond Press, 2001).

Better Than God

As He said of the orchestra
at the Creation, *they can play
anything you put in front of them.*

Buried Abroad

Bert Hinkler, aviator,
born in Bundaberg,
disappeared one day
in the Nineteen Twenties
in the Pratomagno,
found only years later.

His first bi-plane hung
in the Brisbane Museum
while a captured German tank
stood guard outside
to stop imagination
sorting out its dead.

My Father's only brother –
with no known grave in France
or any cache of letters sent
from London back to Brisbane –
suggests his nephew join him
anywhere but home.

The Apprentice's Sorcerer

In Geneva in a plague-deep hole,
Recreating how the universe began,
In heat as keen as God's impulsive plan,
Scientists seek to animate the soul
Of everything that's classified as Life,
Victor Frankenstein's convulsions, Cain's Stanley knife.

Somewhere a little knowledge starts to gesture.
It may be dangerous but it's enterprise;
It levels difference in weight and size;
Its beauty is of skin and not in vesture –
This is the secret of the lead made gold,
The bread from stone, a timeless Paradise on hold.

The world looks on: so Paracelsian
Such hubris and such cost! What is there still
To do to prove Creation's codicil?
And is this Back to Basics or Caesarian
To keep your figure, as the Magi squat
Around the Electronic Crib at Santa's Weinacht Grot.

Apprentices galore have heard the call –
Ives' and Stevens's Insurance days,
Pascal's mathematics second-guessed as praise,
Hopkins' Ignatian Exercises stalled.
Many have shunned the rules to get to grips
With a broadband innovation of Apocalypse.

Empowered by forces somehow empathised,
A personal or general Crusade
May go awry: the pendant legal blade
Reflecting love of Reason and its prized
And ironising power may fall on throats
Which called for Joachim's Heaven or Universal Votes.

Each innovator served an inner voice
Superbly iterating sounds of Truth,
Some from a lifetime's wisdom, some from youth,
And none believing they had any choice –
But who among these bristling handers-down
Of the Aurora of New Birth knew verb from proper noun.

Perhaps in this Swiss Hole the world will see
A proof beyond its statutory Big Bang
And hear that what the Morning Angels sang
Was more than some wide-screened banality.
The love which moves the sun and the other stars
Is syntax-negligent, and may never parse.

We do Not Write the Way We Are

My Mother was more a Small Investor
than she was Queen Clytemnestra
but she bought me shares in dreams,
in doing not what is, but seems –
you start out rhyming, she declared,
but go your own way into dread
　　　with bed sores and bad words.

Orestes' and Electra's Mum
was, in their view, the Higher Scum.
I loved my Mother and I tried
to feel less guilty, so I cried,
but in those dreams she willed me have
I dug around her missing grave –
　　　now write that up, she said.

I do not write the way I am,
I rode on a storm when I sat in a tram,
my fears were highly rational
but only when I dreamed – The Fall
was daily life, the Workers' Wheel,
the tangled web we're told we weave,
　　　the millions historied.

How do we scan the things we write?
Is this our fabled Second Sight,
the huge reflective Self interred
in generations of the Word?
I'd love to pose as Terrorist
or Trotsky under House Arrest,
　　　but sadly I'm not mad.

Instead, a circumstantial Truth
without the vanity of proof
is mixing in my double mind
with darkness lining up behind,
an unfree kind of Free Trade Zone,
a Fascist rule insisting words
       report to me alone.

The Downside

And the small exemplary lives
for which great cathedrals were constructed
are with us still. Here is the incinerator
your Father burned his leaves in –
there is the great book of the Inferno
where hate has a part for everyone,
perhaps you had a hand in it?
It goes on being written – on the other side,
as people say. Once you have a calling
you know you will be called for.

Moi à l'Égard du Je

To write your history of Janus
Imagine the dual parts of Self,
The Head defected from the Anus,
Kindness on stand-by, Prurience
Brought down a peg from its Top Shelf
And Judgement sitting on the fence.

Thus, capitalised, the halves of You
Can find excuses for their chill
Indifference to the Human Crew
And watch unmoved the world go by.
Ice is forming on the sill,
A cold Me with regard to I.

Anything more than Two's a crowd
But I and Me are company;
What's not compelled shall be allowed.
The Questioner who sits so sly
Is I one moment, then it's Me
And Me has turned my face from I.

Whereof We Cannot Speak

There is nothing here 'whereof'. We are
philosophers and drainmakers,
prospectus-holders, vainly gripping
the under-edge of a minor star.

On which we know we can't stay quiet.
How many sonnets must we write
before the great gong sounds in Heaven?
And is this calm a call to riot?

A species which feels sorry for
not just itself, but worms and bats,
would like to make life fair and take
the wrinkles out of sex and war.

Under the microscope it seems
to be covered in odd parasites
called words, and like the pigeon must
talk to walk, nodding at dreams.

Self-lecturing, it fills the Hall
with topoi and parameters
and delegates with names on badges
fulminating where they sprawl.

The brain floats on a lake of words,
just as once the world was held
on elephant-back above a sea –
subversive rhyme suggests that herds

Of metaphors with sharper beak
tear at the silence of unease:
a philosopher feels on his cheek
the tears whereof he cannot speak.

Because We Can

This sensation
We say is the nation
Acting its destiny.
How like is it
To the smaller act which here we see,
The incomplete Devil paying a visit?

We know it is our
Fate to lack power –
Is this our excuse
That we are very small
Among demagogues whose job is to choose
The Few's good or the Good of All?

Perhaps at home
Thought might roam
In rhyme's paradigm
From native spite
In bed or drawing room to Real Time
Downloaded to us day and night.

Should then we ask
To whom the task?
There have been, we know,
Unflinching souls
Who've travelled far as thought can go.
Why is the world dying between the poles?

Nobody today,
At least down our way,
Slaves in mines
Or starves or freezes,
Yet each Old Baron in his Saturnines,
In the market's name, does as he pleases.

Oh come off it –
It's only Profit,
One of our boasts,
Free Will for Man!
We bitumen the fields and flood the coasts
Because we must because we can.

Anger's Anger-Management

Described Depression as the New Self-Pity,
Agreed our lions still are donkey-led,
Wished Asbos on the Turner Prize Committee,
Screened female columnists with precise distaste,
Winced at clubbers jetting to the Med:
Was seen at Paddington, rabid and red-faced.

Took the Discipline Cure, shouting at the News,
Tried to dissect the syntax-shape of meaning,
Found in dreams which turns will fit which screws,
Feared madness in late afternoon, and fury
Of an Only Child's protracted weaning
And acted Hanging Judge to Venal Jury.

A Resurrection

The rising is preserved in alabaster;
what if dreams might equally be saved?
Would we have a whole doxology
of horror tailored to each person's need?
A sumptuous belief is beckoning
in sculptured incarnation, as those muscles
take the strain, those bulging eyes find joy
in stone resuscitation, and the God
of this inertia joins his effigy.

That War is the Destruction of Restaurants

All occasions bloom within priorities.
Insensible and more insensible selves
Choose to marry in their most-frayed cuffs.

They are promising riches in the Afterlife
Where every thread unravelling is a star
Within a plain of anecdotal stars.

This is the only true intelligence
Of taste: you open eyes in infancy
And see a dog in death-throes from a bait.

The prunus clipped, a glorious parent and
A fearful one speak of themselves at tea.
The five-foot line is waiting to usurp.

Like God, our animators are upset
By nought on nought, always too many noughts –
Stop dying now, they say to Dacca floods.

In Pantheons the heroes may not snore
Or be androgynous in twilight tombs
Since sexual peace is firmly cut in stone.

Year on year the wars arrive and raze
The science plains: we want to order fire
And do so staring at the plat-du-jour.

The Immemorial Dove

It sang outside all night, the dove
in the sarcophagus, not the owl,
singing for everyone, not just to a High Priest
from above or to set itself in hieroglyph,
but burbling nicely in dream-dying,
the dove of qualifications, the if-
and-when bird, singing on a wire
or steeple, of responsibility,
of death and life tonight, and what will be.

An easy reminder to forget at dawn
when light's own noises fill the frame
and Nature wakes Anxiety on the bed.
If everything's a warning, let us read
the score – the dove's coo an *Hauptstimme*,
warmest of trills the poet recognized
as murmurings of innumerable Bs –
another note will do as well to end
not just a life but living's confidence.
Then let the dove descend chromatically
beyond its usual allegory
down its eleven channels to become
the balsam and bereavement of the earth.

To Murder Sleep

I'll dream another worst tonight,
The perfect lines I'll never write,
Some much-applauded dumbing-up
The Gold Experimental Cup,
And prompted by my certainty
Burn form in its own effigy.

The world is forcing us to show
That relevance may not go slow,
That what might fit is not allowed,
That 'Art To Go' will please the crowd
While self-elected Prophets dwell
In Academia's arc-en-ciel.

Dovetailed with fears of seventy years
A ghostly furniture appears;
It moves with ease from prototype
To fearful dream – its mode is hype,
Panopticon of all that's new,
It gleams in Weekend interview.

And now it beckons me to sleep
And break the rules I try to keep.
'Remember, you were crazy once,
You're still both Neophile and Dunce,
So outperform on death's trapeze
Your competence of enemies.'

No Heaven Cold Enough

Suddenly the worlds of death and substance seem to pause
in their mechanical obedience to the rules of time

And tension: we, the holders of Philosophy's new Bibles,
look away from everything we know corrodes, and speak

Pentecostally if cautiously of the Plan of Man, the engines
of his mind's consistency, the freedom from delay his towers

Know, forever rising from cartographies of hope!
But the ghost which Yeats would revel in will not be sent

Out naked on the roads for punishment – no element
may carry life's prefigured comical audacity

Beyond its blood-veiled site: nothing waiting on this moment
or this pen will freeze the spirit to a mind-free shape.

A Very Forgiving Medium

Our landlord's man has let us off this time,
    We're not expelled.
Victorians liked their mortar made with lime,
    Our walls have held.

A very forgiving medium, it seems,
    Not like cement
Which struts and strangles until roofs and beams
    Are racked and rent.

Round here the jerry-built and stucco'd blocks
    From Hardy's Age
Have huge exciting windows, paradox
    Of bird and cage

Whose first proprietors sang by coal-fires
    The servants set,
Whose morals were adjacent their desires
    To have and get.

Their cold-faced world turned them to optimists;
    However hard
To be In Trade and climb the Social Lists,
    The Visiting Card

Was trusted to revoke Equality,
    That careless turn
Which might mean daughters' tears, a son at sea,
    The ash-filled urn.

Their slapdash heirs, rent-paying Arrivistes
        From anywhere,
Prefer a nervous vigil to a feast,
        And stair by stair

Mount to a tower where their metered gaze
        Tracks modern living,
A limeless medium, fallen on hard days
        And unforgiving.

The Dead Have Plans

They have missed their chances of becoming gods
But are left with the consolation of words.
They'd have liked to be controllers of tides.

They can hear still the living talking of passions
And comfortable heirs comparing pensions,
Recounting the while their favourite positions.

Perhaps three score and ten is only half a loaf
But who would measure all the waste in his life?
Crematoria can burn merely some of the stuff.

Once dead any half-decent line will seem poetry
And 'pretty well' may pass for priority.
You're no longer tied to your pituitary.

Strong Men, Weak Men and Middle-of-the-Road Men
Insist they're bored by the 'Condition of Man',
Saying, 'Can't you put in more parsley and cumin?'

The Dead hear the trees inside their coffins
Sigh to the wind the eight Dalmatic Questions –
Must it all start again, the leaking equations?

They fear the mirror they walk through is clouding,
There's nothing either side, and only colluding
Will keep the living and the dead from colliding.

The Little Fish Have Gone

The little fish had twinkling bright red fins,
could turn on a five-pence piece,
never needed to pretend
that artificial plants are edible
or Science is a watery god,
a fons-et-origo out of the tap.

And the big fish are looking guilty.
The morning census bides a tear
and the people of the house
are momentarily gods.

Young Mothers in the Square

How long is it since I, as them,
An old rose on a branching stem,
Kept watch through cloudy grass and sun
That no harm come to anyone
In this Our Pale, yet might deplore
The garden as a metaphor
Where married love dies intestate
En route to some half-hopeful date.

Each Mother her own Queen of Sheba
Arrives sans Scottie or Retriever –
NO DOGS ALLOWED – the apple-trees
As young as any one of these
Are unconcerned by all increase
Or denim well above the knees.
We breed an Economic Race
With angels at the Interface.

A shadow falls across the lawn;
Is it the poet's unearned scorn?
How can they play, as Gray observed,
Unconscious of their fate? The curved
Blades of their death swing round
Like frisbees looping to the ground
Where everything is burgeoning,
A rose, a laptop, someone's bling.

An Azalea Armada

We, the besieged, pray quietly on the porch
For real light and not this sultry subterfuge
So out of place in midday's sempiternam.
O flowers burning in a bush, we've lost
Our sense of liturgy, or if we have it,
It must be for the dead the landscape holds.
Quam olim Abrahae promisisti, yet
Is any Requiem worth the finishing?

The Room is Sane

This is the truthful 'beam-me-up-and-down' pad,
The only time-turf between the galaxies
And allegory's complacent everywhere.
Its verbs are clipped to having, not to had;
Its notes, how widely ranging, surge to Cs;
Its heavenly ladder is a step downstairs.

Chief City of the Marches, it has seen
Fast-changing battles, so won't fly a flag;
No plaques upon a wall would stand for Justice;
Explorers' words, curt portage and careen,
Are on its blog; time won't speak or drag;
Its halcyon is rinsed from what's amiss.

It censors all supporting anecdotes,
Blocked drains of childhood, prime unhappiness
Aspiring to the Classic, burgled sex –
Your party life, though buried beneath coats,
Has pledged you to this room, the one address
Where Oedipus still claims the title Rex.

A Minatory Submission

Desire for excessive carnal love
never truly leaves the human body.

Basil the Eremite

Desire to overcome the vanity
Of soul is what drives humans on to sex –
Just so the mariners of an Inland Sea
Declare when shown the ocean's vast complex.
We are so inward that we find ourselves
Matching bits of bodies from top shelves:
I see my partner; nobody sees me.

There was a room. In it a Major said
To a female aide returned from R and R:
'What do I want? You, naked in my bed!
The war won't end; not here nor any star
Will harbour peace or comfort risen flesh;
Our one recycling is forever fresh.
Who structured love intended this instead.'

Chocolates and Gratitude

The subject of this poem is 'top shelf'
Though ever since the Latins and the Greeks
Sex has been where power shows itself,
An alternating current, lows and peaks,
And human consciousness, a common prude,
Unwilling to confront its self-parade,
Has found a kind of profane servitude
In setting Nature up as Christian Aid.

Sex demands its tribute as the one
Ever-interesting topic; having begun
With what the magazines dilate upon –
Mistresses performing what wives shun,
Or giving it, expect both chocolates
And gratitude – our argument insists
What academics know: the later poems of Yeats
Are the sublimation of ageing pessimists.

Commercial truth which Marx said underwrote
The Trojan War extends beyond mere lust
To trading which does best where people vote.
Pascal got omens wrong, since Helen's bust
Not Cleopatra's nose provoked a war
Whose potent sign on T-shirts of the young
Promoted love as hardly known before,
A world-wide-web on which lost lives are strung.

Instincts and their Viciousest Toads*

Our good Saint Freud has kept us Germanised,
not yet Illusion of the Future, but also not
detached from Onkel Hegel's apron-strings.

Which toad is this? A church toad settling for
the sinner's vision of repentance, a wounded
Prince of Sorrows in his Monsalvat?

The science toad: the Watcher on the Islands
observing lizards parse their legs and colours
while sun remains unchanged in diorite?

Bufo philosophicus, language-dribbler
that never dreams, is always hungry and
commands the talk at tyrants' banqueting?

The devil toad that's wicked only as
make-weight to God's fixed pendulum
but asks to serve in Miss Moore's deathly garden?

The toad which sat on Larkin, strangely marked
and hating leisure more than work? Would it
squat for its photo on Desire's grave?

Fiercest of all, unkillable Cain toad
which has so many brothers and which sees
a million greenings through the canopy?

Though all are born to perish as the sparks
fly up and downwards, participators know
that words are harmless lights to trick the sky.

No toad would need to know a word. The scene
is always Toad Hall, family-seat. Take one
instinctive look around you – do you see?

* See Sigmund Freud's 1915 essay *Triebe und Triebschiksale*, translated into
English as *Instincts and their Vicissitudes*.

Leafing Through the Latin Dictionary

Fuga, fugas – music now, not back
at school where Harry Roberts flashed his gown,
a toga to berate a class as slack
as Rome became; we'd been meant to be
English Augustans, but were soon brought down
to being worthy only of a few
emotive Saxon nouns and verbs: the sea
had brought our fathers to a sanded shore,
packed tight with iron sermons on The Poor –
but still the dictionary had work to do:
peregrinus, wanderers in need
of some Virgilian outcome – might this book
have shown how Europe's words could safely bleed
on strands Aeneas left to Captain Cook?

Oppidanus – not from Rome, but not
from Eton either; if from anywhere
we hailed from pissed-on concrete and caked snot,
a gravel-rash battalion called up for
training in Real Estate and prostate snips –
no worse for that, but somewhere off there lurked
a world whose words were from a greater law,
the Pax Britannica, a king in sight,
an Empire wider than a day and night,
the home boys set to die among the ships –
spero, spes – we hoped, and now it's here,
the Trading-Up Republic, confident
of its own sparky Roman atmosphere
and *timeo*, to fear the gifts we're sent.

Under the Rupe Tarpeia

How many years ago was it I learned,
Half-interested, about the rock from which
The Romans tossed their traitors? Now this pitch
Is what I look at: having missed the road,
I've doubled back, my set-self half-returned
To giving answers in a school-boy mode.

Fatigue however terse is all you feel
On classic pilgrimage since they are dreams
These real places, and as soon as seems,
Are replicas; the shed blood condescends
To test al fresco which is the more real,
The death below the rock, the talk of friends.

The path winds round so smoothly it negates
Precipitation; onwards, not so sheer,
The back door of the Capitol is near
And then the toothless Forum comes in view
And Severus or Constantine orates
Out of time to cats and Christ and you.

The scene reminds you, you must make the leap,
That how you live does not provoke the law.
What Rome is now is what Rome was before.
First Person Pronoun, authorised to rule,
Looks at the Rock and asks, 'If death is deep,
Why does the fall appear so minuscule?'

Horace Takes the Waters

Odes 3.13

This spring which seems concurrent glass,
Bandusia, with flowers amid
Its wine-bright eddies, smiles on us
As if it knows that here a kid
With little peering snail-like horns
Tomorrow shall be sacrificed.

A death to crown both love and war
But all in vain: the blood will tip
Into the icy stream a store
Of wanton crimson, staining all
That lives and grows, the flocks that sip,
The generations of the grass.

Though dog-star Sirius bares his teeth
Upon the scorching Summer air,
His brittle snarl, which all beneath
The sky cringe from, shall lose its force
Where wandering herds and ploughman share
The water's chill beneficence.

Of legendary fountains, none
Will be so cherished as this place
Where living lace descends and sun
Commands the ilex tree to brush
The water's enigmatic face
And picture immortality.

Voltaire's Allotment

All Paris is a banlieu, as all
    Cities everywhere are vile
        As written to by St Paul.

Therefore what I choose to cultivate,
    Like an attendant servant's smile,
        Is the allotment of debate.

Those small sections tucked behind
    Pantheons and the Monarch's Mile
        Are death warrants yet unsigned.

They are not properly gardens,
    Have no reticulating tile
        Or Le Nôtre's marching margins.

Meanwhile, in the theatre and in pages
    Of classically clanking style
        I circulate for fame and wages.

What I sow is European opinion,
    Shallots to tingle and beguile,
        Not the full apocalyptic onion.

Sitting at a liberal ruler's board,
    Talking hangman's talk the while,
        I strip notes from the common chord.

Finally, for my bequest, I leave
    A new church, 'a sumptuous pile',
        And, duly on Revolution's eve,

As reliquary of Rousseau,
    The tears of Europe in a phial
        And the allotments where they grow.

Detoxing Dante

He knew the azure sky was Heaven-dressed

Like Tuscan cruelty and the Tuscan tongue,
A language for all Italy and soon
A text for scholar-dogs to roll upon.

Perhaps he envied each unhappy wraith
Rising from the turbulence of Hell
Since in his hands not even rhyme was safe,

So they're immortalised by what they tell
And we who read can guess they're pleased to be
In shit if there's no other place to dwell.

Alas, it comes down to complicity;
Poets harangue and bully and confess
And feign to publish through eternity.

The dictionary folds them to her breast.

In Bed with Oblomov

I know you'd rather sleep alone,
Ilya Ilyich, but you are safe with me,
   As I am Sleep myself, your own
Entitlement to common harmony
   And I can promise you no dream
Will trouble you – like pretty women who
   Are also nice, or friends who seem
True friends, yet truly too good to be true,
   Or servant faithful in her heart,
A cook as simple and as scrupulous
   As porridge, or the teasing art
Of *Casta diva*, or the endless fuss
   Of paying visits before noon
Or obligations running with the clock –
   Let these be banished like the moon,
You are with me; that bang was not a knock!
   Beyond your windows Russia sleeps
In snow, as drifts, which may not even be,
   Surround your resting; vacant deeps
Soul-white but bled into the wintersea,
   So many ice-bound paper ports
Which Czars have deemed our Western Doors
   While civil servants class the sorts
Of overdue reforms we stall by wars.
   Give up the world, even when awake,
Attain a glorious discontinuancy
   Where sunlight is a guilty fake –
Let someone clean the room, but be with me

At drowsing's edge and share the dust
Which lullabies the noise of coach and street.
    Pull blankets up, give it your trust,
This love-bed made for just one pair of feet.

Money and Stravinsky

A Duologue

MONEY: Mine is the measure and the turbulence,
                        An orthodoxy piloting the earth,
                        The gelling and the using of inheritance,
                        First irritation at an Afterbirth,
                        Academy of everything which ranges –
                        Ermine and hyperbole of manges.

STRAVINSKY: Sergei and I kept Russia in our tread
                        And like Turgenev's sympathy with serfs
                        We passed our Liberalism to the dead:
                        Ustilug and Petersburg were turfs.

MONEY: The world's a chaos only I can smoothe.
                        Marvell and Pushkin, one convivial,
                        The other like a gland, knew how to soothe
                        The world's antinomy: what each might sell
                        He'd hide away from light. Money alone
                        Sits under the candelabra on its throne.

STRAVINSKY: All over Europe history requires
                        From promissory notes, too brashly given,
                        Both salon-lit and adamantine fires,
                        But who will pay the mortgage on such Heaven?

MONEY: I grant you you were not so absolute
                        As those green German giants, Fafner-like,
                        Who stood there guarding myths and almost mute
                        Inside their engine noise. 'Get on your bike',
                        I said, 'Composing with Twelve Notes will keep
                        You banking while the tall conductors sleep.'

STRAVINSKY: He said, 'She's deaf'; I said, 'This deafness pays.'
My music never asks what wealth prefers;
While making judgement truthfulness purveys
Through tears how fast Cocteau's mascara blurs.

MONEY: It's relaxation time inside the Fisc
As Swiss concerns survive another way.
Let's look at Art, the picture and the disc –
Each Nobel glory of the year before
Is ancient news, while innovation stalls,
Strapped in a vault or on a banker's walls.

STRAVINSKY: They said I loved you, served you all too well –
'Whatever my agent says . . .' my every sin
Dies at the keyboard. How compose the smell
Of Classicism rotting in its skin?

MONEY: Nobody's inspiration, so I'm told,
Merely the means of buying time to write,
Yet Timon, lost to Nature, dug up gold
The better to watch the whores and generals fight.
A metaphor that's more a catalyst,
I help invent whatever would exist.

STRAVINSKY: You press me on my weakness – why not look
Into the hottest crucible of all,
My parsimonious mind? Judas forsook
His Master. What Bach did was read the wall.

MONEY: The studio manager in cans rotates
His arms to wind us up – some cutaways
Before the Hospitality Room debates.
Our blacks and reds fade off to even greys.
The world is made of such retentive stuff
None in the break-up ever gets enough.

STRAVINSKY: If evil has a root then music must
As Life's most abstract shoot acknowledge it.
The wind sweeps past the Steppes and still the dust
Blows to the Neva; the fittest serve the fit.

Henry James and Constipation

The mail creeps into Florence with the sun
And I, along these lotus-lettered tiles,
Touch at the door of Disappointment; smiles
Of fellow-guests I am ashamed to shun
Adorn the corridors and I assume
The living William's in a letter in my room.

Your strictures, William, if I call them thus,
Are Medical Injunctions, similar
To that one body-mind self-avatar
We hold is Moral Truth. The impetus
Of our distinct decorums, like our bowels,
Stays with the Signoria and the men with trowels.

Why do we quit our shores of sense to seek
Something no better, but much longer known?
Their mason's trowels! We think, perhaps we've sown
The present with the past. Is Boston weak
In wanting to declare a glorious pose
Just truths a waiter winks or scholar might disclose?

Dear Henry, says the word-within-the-words,
You've eaten Europe, now digest it well:
Alice, yourself, all Jameses should dispel
Inheritance, as migratory birds,
Wingspanned enough, approach the classic coasts
Of Excellent Ambush, hangman's shadows, faction's ghosts.

The pills are packed, small dictionaries of hope,
Encyclopaedias encroaching on
The atlas where the motorist may swan
The shore. Old Europe's by new Huxleyan soap
Made clean. One half-Swiss hint from Burckhardt and
All art lies open like an oyster in the hand.

In Rome one day at Carnival a flour-
Bomb surprised me, covering me in white,
A proper suiting for the Church of Night,
If somewhat vulgar. Climb the tallest tower,
View any landscape here, its sepulture
Is cold retention, derogated, anal, dure.

De Quincey had my trouble – opium
For him; for me, inaction, looking on,
The bathroom stalled, the crucial moment gone.
The Bread of Culture, eaten crumb by crumb,
Chokes off all other appetite, and we
Who will one day be prints exist in effigy.

The picture of itself, the Great Good Land,
Which waits your passage in the sired boat,
Is not so truthful as a brother's coat,
Your many-coloured words. We understand
Each other who were not made here, but seek
The broad bestowing stream fed by clearskin creek.

The mail leaves town, I've often noted, by
The Porta Roma, wheels retarded, carrying
Enchantments far back home, the marrying
And dying, gossiping – this claimed life's wry
Postmark of ancient love and new device
Is Advent of Degree, point made, distinction nice.

Agape at Albi

Somewhere in this pink and hairless monster
is the flea of God which bites and sucks and wants
to die, as you will soon. Which is why
its walls are covered with emblems, sculptures, abstracts,
all in service of Euclidean Divinity,
the opposite of everything which suffers and infests.
In this *carcere* of souls the animation is
from history, an iconography too crude
to tempt a louse out on a collar, while the Choir's
a stall for the more angelic animals
at the abattoirs. We visit here and celebrate
Correction's flogging-post which La Pérouse,
Albi's second-best celebrity, observed
at Sydney Cove, a transferred massacre.
'God will know his own', my flea might guess,
comfortable in discrete specifics,
pledging that every stab and draught of blood
should prove a rare transcendence, one the pink
and parenthetic walls must tolerate,
their agape a rosary of bites.

Birds in the Garden of
the Cairo Marriott

And you, little birds, are waiters but not smiling,
hopping at the sad indignity of that man
(he said Detroit was home) on his second
giant burger; with your quick in-and-out
besieging tables sweetened by the sugared sky
of Cairo, you mock the nicest men with napkins
on their shoulders – would they snap at scraps? –
and your big rivals, we'd call them crows
but they are dignity itself in brown tuxedos,
peering from high perches of a Disney Ramasseum,
speaking faultless American forever,
they must be Prefects of the Underworld!

The little dust we drop our crumbs upon
seethes like the Red Sea Crossing – if this is history,
asks a powerless nation, can mere birds
patrol the Valley of the Kings each morning?
Three sparrows who have 'hotep' somewhere
as a suffix drop beside our just uncovered
breakfast tomb: all food, they say,
is like another wave upon the Nile, a dream
worth sleeping for – the gods immured in obelisks
consider everything; their High Priests clad in aprons
are opening umbrellas as the sun begins
to climb above the masts of potted palms.

When Did You Last See Castagno?

Welcome to the feast, *piccolo pasero*,
A feast that never ends, of loyalty and treachery –
Two are sold for a farthing, little sparrow.

How did you get in, confront the tracery
Beyond the boarded-up high window
To fly so gaily past the painted sky?

Five hundred years ago the roughest of the rough
Wooed the nuns to let his fingers show
The meal where Christ dared God to call his bluff.

Andrea from Monte Falterona, so
Much the shepherd boy still, with your rack
Of dangling bodies striping the Bargello.

The living have to eat, though Christ's quick snack
Speaks of digestion moving to its end.
Judas eyes up God: on us he turns his back.

A sparrow would know how to eat his friend:
Such is the law in this Cenacolo.
A bird's wings tempt the angels to descend.

The team with Christ is all Italo-Sure,
Captains of Refreshment, whereas you,
Small sparrow, are God's cynosure.

You might have watched Castagno with his colours
Through light which faded while you flew. Since then
The world has been defined behind closed doors.

A poet's choice, a sparrow, not a wren,
His rhyme uncertain like a painted loaf,
With Life as Art and Art as regimen.

How will you find your way out now you're in?

Glumdalclitch's Cleavage

Though I walk in the Valley of the Shadow of Death
I will fear only the metaphors of fear,
I have found a keeper more incautious than myself.

She is this gentle giant (Oh the joy of using decently
a journalistic cliché), a twelve-year-
old inhabitant of Brobdingnag, a mere child.

She is the picture I have now of God – power with
love, concern with system, looks without veneer,
a strength which worries at its carefulness.

Doctors say I'm hoist on my own dreams.
I ride upon a nipple, I abseil down an ear.
What is small in me is remade large in them.

My arcane pictures of philosophy and war
which shocked their king, nevertheless appear
in the skin of each of these: their stretched world

Is shadowed forth in me, but oh my tender nurse
I never had at home an inkling of that queer
solicitude, your scientific starch.

Lifelong I've been surrounded by immensity
and sung and prayed it in the heavenly sphere,
Mr Addison's 'spacious firmament on high'.

But I was cowering from such optic wit –
where would I go to hide? And now it's clear
that safe in Glumdalclitch's breasts I've reached

The one defile denied spoiled Lucifer –
how could he tell the far-off from the near
or guess divinity in a choice of metaphor?

Strontium to Mendeleyev

What joy to meet you, Dmitri Ivanovich,
In this your Periodic Chancellery.
My more than seven times seventy years' itch
Is a consummation devoutly to be wished:
I sit at the table you have laid for me.

Number and Rank! Mass 87 plus,
Thirty-eighth from Father Hydrogen,
And yet I turn your children's milk to pus.
They call it valency when we discuss
How murderous this numbered regimen.

O Governor from God, Profound Encoder,
Whose agents are the elements of earth,
Instinct us well, Harmonius Downloader,
Entrope our restlessness, as hairy Yoda
Disciplined that boy of astral birth.

Dostoyevsky's Flat, St Petersburg

Refurbish Dostoyevsky's gloomy flat!
Apocalypse as heating under floor,
Madness steaming in a samovar,
A cat on cushions watching for a rat.

We love to put ourselves in others' shoes
And hope to meet them in their words and sounds –
Milhaud's scores thrown out with coffee grounds,
Incestuous carpets plump Miss Austen's Muse.

Enormous forests force Chekhov to ride
With nowhere to call home; stern Faulkner likes
A brothel's morning quiet; Chausson bikes
Up to death; and Webern steps outside.

Not much a connoisseur can do with these
Too shapely instances – perhaps we play
With celebrated trivia to allay
A sense of loss, of purloined apogees.

It takes us back to Dostoyevsky's flat
To try to meet Raskolnikov and trace
The Christ lines mixing on Prince Myshkin's face
And watch voracity burn off its fat.

Shakespeare's Defeat

No one has ever been his equal
Yet quizzing him in doggerel
Is any Tribune's timid right:
All language is dispersed in light.

The Ordinary sunk in ordinariness
Say he is bald and hard to guess.
The Archons think to find a focus
Might tear its petals from the crocus.

Country Wisdom's top Townee,
His Coat of Arms Complicity –
The bubo of the world when squeezed
Is odium, yet some are pleased.

The Adam Smithy of our need
Commands both vile and pedigree'd.
So Mouldy, Feeble and Bullcalf
Get pricked: the audience gets to laugh.

His works are like Miss Emin's tent –
She sleeps with all, not just the bent,
But stencilled on the flapping walls
Legitimation calls and calls.

Music does it better, so
He has a journey shortly to go
But never come to that fine palace
Up a beanstalk from the phallus.

We writers want him as our Prince
The crazy public to convince
But would he even place a bet
On redemption via the Internet?

The dark house and detested wife:
After marriage, get a life!
Start out defeated – the glory is
Your Art shall seem victorious.

George Crabbe at 'The White Hart'

Here steppeth out the Old Saltmaster's Son
To unrefine respectability.
He lets them guess he's scheming poetry;
An ounce of living yet may weigh a ton.

At Slaughden he discovered Verse can paint
All Nature in the hues of Paradise –
An inverse Paradise of course, where Vice
Enjoys the pure indifference of a Saint.

He's always been as healthy as a tree –
The sap ascends, the bark is left behind
And sheep-bells tuned in thirds and fifths remind
A tone-deaf poet of Life's poverty.

Lost Among the Lizards

To ask yourself do lizards ever dream
Will entertain a burning afternoon
As uselessly as any other theme

You might cull out of thought. You say the moon
Has served its misanthropes as perch
To set despair out, stage a night cartoon

Of Nineteenth-Century divine research,
The ever-loving, ever-seeing eye
Of what kept faith when at a fatal lurch

The Sun of Sureness seemed to fail the sky
And fireflies eclipsed along the sad
Margins of Leopardi's dream might try

To be the stars of everything which had
A place in melancholy. To be old
Was horror, but to be still young was mad.

Yet, why, before the afternoon grows cold,
Bring out the moon to simplify a state
Of nervousness, the often oversold

Imagination of the temperate
When faced with living's ordinary misrule,
The scuttling lizards halted in template?

Such groundling geckos might have watched the cruel
Death of Cicero, but no tragedy
Burns long enough to justify its fuel.

There was, they knew, no mystery to see
Other than something coming to an end,
A change of topos, ways of yet to be.

The lizards, Empson might have said, 'perpend',
But what do they perpend? A balance in
Whose other pan our feeling selves descend?

To dress now in myself, my sun-drenched skin,
I should confess I might be happy here
In mountains where the sun will flash a fin

Around the peaks or suddenly appear
A half self-conscious Phaeton riding on
A wave of mist, too surf-bound stiff to steer,

But now the circuit of my mind has gone
Behind the burning light; I cannot feel
That warm-limbed, lizard-like phenomenon

Of living in the real world, the real
Unpersuaded territory where
No truths impose, no needs can break their seal.

In which way am I lost? What I might share
In lizard literature would be world-wide
Apocalypse: we'd suction off the air

Which sweetens garden paths; we'd hide
Our fears along pink warmths of stone,
Praise Valkyries of butterflies which ride

The hero-path as each flower dies alone;
We'd say we know the source of every scream
And pitch our ears to dying's monotone.

Lizard Anthropomorphism – now the dream
Can be made true; this beauteous quadruped
Sits in my hand and wonders do I seem

A sentient creature with too big a head,
Semi-articulated limbs and eyes
Which cannot scan and look inwards instead.

It will not tell its dream and if I'm wise
I'll break into a book where living is
Forever independent of surprise

Or fate of morning plans, the *hers* and *his*
Of modern understanding, fearful hearts
Lost in the words of their periphrasis.

A perfect loss! And as the evening starts
To lure the lizards back behind the vine
And stinging flies locate uncovered parts

Of limbs, the soul is mercantiled by wine,
An exiled iPod chronicles a tune
And nothing of this various world is mine.

To John Ashbery

In the end, aren't you a bit pissed
at living in the world's most powerful country?

Wouldn't you rather, like the Late Roman Poets,
coruscate in the margins of a worn-out Empire?

Or is it better to watch the selvedge fray
of a homeland with a retail future?

It's the close-ups which matter, I'm sure you'd agree.
So sickening, so beautiful, such filigree.

Vita Somnium Breve

It could be by Old Smoothie Suckling
But it *is* a picture by Böcklin,
A painter unfashionable now,
Swiss German, precise, middlebrow.

Tempera on mahogany base,
Ill-behaved 'Death' in your face,
Two babies with flowers by a stream,
To a Fred or a Freud, just a dream.

A warrior horsed with aplomb,
A girl shows the crack in her bum,
A skeleton lashes a man –
Cram forensics in where you can.

But why does this painting, I ask,
Make me think of a poet who basked
In the Avant-Garde's gestural playing
And ended, a case of self-slaying?

Where love broke her words into pain
French Theorists looked on in vain
And Cambridge kept turning its back,
Its sneers rising stack upon stack,

The death-current now filled her head,
The Lethe in spate through her bed,
What else but take Verse out of pawn
And leave Barthes and *Tel Quel* forlorn.

Poor Veronica, no napkin to place
Across her blue-eye-shadowed face.
Her Language Games ended like this –
Into the arms of (quote) gloomy Dis.

So weep for a scholar who cloned
Tennyson, Swinburne and Pound
And followed her gift and left home
To live in High Culture alone.

When Böcklin depicts Life's Brief Dream
He asks us to follow his theme:
To Veronica breasting the line
Death whispers there's still enough time.

The Burning Fiery Furnace

Born to a seamless ordinance of heat,
Small wonder I best remember Indoors,
The too-small carpets slipping round the floors
And 'Under the House', a region to retreat

To for the many guilty dreams of peace,
An 'enfer' where the shards of poetry
Shared a complicit afterlife with me –
The Rome of Brisbane, the Annerley of Greece.

But classicism isn't quite the point.
I was in a crucible. I know it now
And can't regret it – will God Speed the Plough
To bring my Father to the Sunday joint?

Henry Ford was right: what's history,
Why do Australians wonder who they are?
Infinite stars in heaven – your one star
Is your own life – the millions don't agree.

They sulk in digits and symposia
And measure muscle-tone and their synapses.
Childhood's Tower (not Ivory) collapses.
Eucalyptus is a plain ambrosia.

I write this down I'm sure because I'm old;
The country of my birth's become hot news
And selfishness should always take short views –
My ancestors came out and found no gold.

The world is made again in each of us.
Australian homes are dark to help the sun
Lure children out for democratic fun.
The myopic boy's gazetted an Odysseus.

Not Greece, though; trust the Bible. Weatherboard
And louvres bank the fire. But is it light
Not heat which terrifies? Ahead, the night
Says, 'State your preference, the stake or sword.'

My Parents Were Walking Islands

Yet I had no floater or Laputa
which might seem God, or whatever
when you are six or seven is your idea
of an enskied propounder of inertia,
a sitter-out on the verandah.

They would have had no use for a filter
to reality who were in every way
and every day each one an accepter
of unmelting territories; out and over,
commanding the washing and the mower.

As Sargasso islands slewed to gather
a sweeter wreck of manhood, they'd meander
in their styleless widowed manner
round their only child, surrendering him
to shadows loosed on the verandah.

How the Eureka Stockade Led to Boggo Road Gaol

Two scars upon our nation's face,
     One though esteemed a glory –
The miners, that heroic race,
Stood in Emancipation's place –
     A gaol's another story.

And Robert Porter, England's son,
     Arriving on this shore,
Could find no reason why the sun
Now shining in the South changed one
     Iota of the Law.

He watched the rebels as I think,
     Their freedom a Greek name,
And traced his balances in ink,
Recalling how at home The Clink
     Was gaol and not his game.

He was an architect; his clan
     Was of true British stock,
But why leave Wiltshire if the plan
Did not engross the Wealth of Man?
     And why reface the clock?

After Eureka, colonies
     Got on with making money.
The legends said that worker bees,
Good Aussies, never bent their knees –
     Barometers set sunny.

In Queensland, that new-minted site,
     The convicts had long gone –
No felons blocked colonial light –
When sugar failed at Petrie Bight
     The Porter star still shone.

What does a new-breached land require?
     Deep-water jetties, pubs,
A church in every rural shire,
The wicked pinned down by its spire,
     And Silvertails in Clubs.

So Robert built them and grew rich
     And aped the London styles.
At Boggo Road he raised his pitch,
A brand new gaol the like of which
     Brought Judges out in smiles.

It's all gone now – gaol, stockade,
     The Porters cut to stem.
A moral, is there one? Invade!
Australians know their land was made
     By History for them.

My Great-Grandfather, pioneer,
     May help me to refuse
To praise my country: he made clear
Between New Start and Old Career
     There's nothing much to choose.

Ranunculus Which My
Father Called a Poppy

The flower which gave Browning his worst rhyme
lined my Father's walk to his Paradise Garden
but he took his time.

Not for him the red of Flanders Fields sprung from
his Brother's body steeped in duckboard marl
nor the necrology of the Somme.

Defeat lived in those several petal folds,
that furry stalk and leaf, those half-drenched pinks
and shabby-borrowed golds.

This modest plant served what was mystical in him,
he'd banish eucalyptus yet cherish the paw-paw's
testicular seraphim.

So Europe and Australia grew together in the sun
of his waterless Eden – not snakes but sparrows
he'd kill, had he a gun.

A whole rift valley of regret ran its juiceless way
among the dahlias, salpiglossis, antirrhinums,
sufficient unto any day.

Later, his Nursing Home was steeped in garden gloom,
a shaven lawn devoid of flowers – for ten years
he surveyed it from one room.

Our front gate is open, I watch him hobble-kneed
sifting his inch-long plants from hessian – ranunculus
are hard to grow from seed.

Christmas Day, 1917

Was there fighting near Comines-Warneton that day?
I doubt there were minglings of combatants
In No Man's Land – it was one Christmas too many.
      But it might have been
A good day to die if ever there could be one.
He may have been wounded elsewhere; the salient
Had many names which guesswork could frequent,
      And hospitals between.

Eighty-nine years later two English schoolgirls
On a Flanders outing have used their new cameras
To record in pastel shades the headstone
      Of Private Neville Main.
Did I know my uncle's other name was Vivian?
I was given Neville in his memory. I joined the House
Of Names years after he had left it – not words, not vows,
      Just the invoiced pain.

How extraordinarily neat, well-spaced,
The Prowse Point Military Cemetery is –
How mistaken my memory of my family's memory
      Of these our far-off dead.
Two weren't even born where I thought they were,
My Mother must have been living still at home
When the news came, but she didn't die alone.
      My civilian Father did.

The valiant inscriptions, chiselled out
Or cemented in, the grass's mapping edges,
My Grandaughters' pictured sky, half-blue –
       Everything's still here.
A Belgian Christmas might well have seemed
Like the traditional ones transported to
Australia, though without the surf in view,
       The sun across the pier.

Time and place are real to the After-Dead
Though their inheritors have forgotten who they were.
Out of the plains of Europe come the tall Hussars
       Like brolgas massing.
As thoughts are lightweight, they can reach the sky.
Allow me, startled Uncles, these complaining words:
Both those who stay at home and those who serve
       Are posted missing.

Opus 77

What works you did will be yourself when you
Have left the present, just as everything
The past passed to the present must become
A terrible unstoppable one blend
Of being there (the world) and not to be
(The self). Grow old along with me, the best
Is bet to be – the worst (of course) lack(s) all
Conviction, as the poet mistranscribed,
Storming a grave to satisfy his pride.
They love me, all my words, despite how often
I made fools of them, betrayed them, begged
Forgiveness of them. They are like the million grubs
Which swarm around their Queen. I file them in
Wide boxes where they wait their Master's Voice,
Accusing and defending. A letter plans
To burst in sullen flame, its heat conserved
By what was written once – but chiefly silence
Triumphs under missing banners – death
Will be the one unmentionable
Impossibility. What happened lives
Parenthetically and privately.

It is time to use words to transcend words,
To make a maquette of the ageing soul
Inside the tired body – abstract, oh
So abstract, but the mind anticipates a real
World trimmed like a Park of Dreams, where blood
Is its own sun and where the self is both
The quarry and the hunter. We who made

A better place with Art (if we did well
Or pointlessly) are privileged to bow
And leave and hope to find the courage to
Confront the mad god of the Universe
And honour one more time those rational
Constructions we have loved. No word will bear
A leaf, since we are dying in our roof-top pots;
Our after-lunch inseminations bring
Cries beneath our windows: we should be
Big enough to fit the act of ending,
The sprawling melodrama of Creation,
And be polite enough to stroll away –
None of that poetic braggadocio
Of buggering off quickly: he meant the body
Not the soul, but arrogance still thinks
The flesh will go on listening, and flaunts
The several litanies of Godhead. Be
Like Haydn abandoning his last quartet;
Need neither saving nor redeeming; greet
The world of breathing and the silent world
With the same material gesture – a bed-post
Now the herm of lost vicinity.

What's Playing in Eternity?

And her inscription of despair
affords a little time to listen:
she was devoted to a more
oblivious obsession, yet some days
there would be space for music
and a favourite piece would play
among the circling furniture,
beyond the deafness of drawn curtains.
Strange that I can see them, stepping from
the record sleeve, three nuns in habits,
inhabiting E-Flat,
empowered as angels to command
a truth more generous than love's.

Discs With Everything

Moses had a trusted follower
at a level lower than his interview
who helped to carry down the Decalogue
from Sinai. What's not well-known
is that the tablets this time came
with special offers, if he filled the forms in,
of incisive and assured declensions
of parallel religions from established
and adjacent states – Assyria, Egypt
and a place called Pontus. He shook them out
over his waste-papyrus basket –
they made quite a mess. Nothing, he said,
can match the matchless offers of the Lord.

Later, there were so many unsolicited
additionals to be discounted.
Along with his *Vita Nuova*, Dante
was obliged to include a CD
of extracts from the *Summa Theologica*
and an offer of a year's subscription
to the continuing concordance. *Paradise Lost*
was similarly intruded on
by *Affairs of State* in tiny type
endorsed by Andrew Marvell
on reproduction House-of-Commons-
headed paper. Decades on, *Mein Kampf*
was outweighed by its onanist inclusions.

Today we know that when tomorrow dawns
all separate offers will be off –
a crowded planet's just an insight
into Heaven or its still invisible
other side, as Hell, and souls will be
unseparate as Blake's hushed grains of sand.
But this we cannot feel because we clutch
our own *Complete and Finished Works*
and have been promised readership
and plaudits. Is it my impulsive notes,
my sugared sonnets or my wizened words
you'll love? I have a dusty disc which played
will cry and cry and will not be switched off.

No Infelicitous Phrases Need Apply

That these ring-doves are not related to
The jackass may be some slight short-circuiting.
      We are all descended from
      Genghis Khan, and in this garden
The whole close patterning is seen at once.
Everything is perfect, and of no concern.

All sorts of tyrannies exist: the apple
Grows slow red in a freaky Summer.
      You see the fault of symmetry,
      It excludes the metaphysic
You were planning for your entry into Heaven –
You say farewell to the idea of proving.

This has been an endlessly extended Eden,
As though the same bee fell from the bud
      That saw an angel pass its tree.
      The only ending was made personal –
Which foot might tread the grass flat wasn't
In the haughty blueprint that time round.

If you look intensively at the blocked wistaria
You come close to the phrasing of a Scriabin,
      Or perhaps Byrd's or Chopin's
      Lyric density of weightlessness.
How can tragedy or some malfunctioning
Cross from a cadence to a statued group?

And if the botanists have even finer phrasing
Will tendrils or their wasted cones demur?
        Will any intelligence ever reach
        The furor of a wind-projected leaf?
A tail-feather left by the Ariadne cat
Is the only way to halve a question-mark.

Will there be sufficient here of stuff
We call, if not quite Life, then circumstance?
        This title's like an airy bridge
        Across an ever-widening Bosphorus.
This side, that side, a simple demarcation:
The badinage is bolted to the air.

By Whose Permission Do These Angels Serve?

Though there are laws of Physics and Thermodynamics
there are no enforcers or permit granters. Most of us
don't see the angels, or perhaps what we do not see
is angelic polystyrene, ectoplasm purposefully set
to hold the world in place. This is what transforms
Nature to Theology; there is no logic, no connection
other than angelic holding hands. How otherwise
could the lawful and unfinished cruelty of existence
ring us on a sapphire day with its insistence
on life's invincibility, our being here the product
of continuous evolution? If X is humorous,
can he be also moving? If emotionally profound,
will Y still be inventive? And now Z calls on some
prosthetic angel to move in mordant dreams
to close his grave up; he sees in strangers' faces
the fellow-candour of a trap. Angels should not be named –
beside a sea, at castle top, in poems by named poets –
they are the air which helps invisibility
to thicken, and have to serve so no angelic waste
might threaten Heaven. Easy to imagine angels
as flamingos wading in a lake, and quite like God,
being neighbourly and pink each day at dawn.

The Judgement of Cambyses

This must be a page from The Manual
For the Instructing of Humanity,
Showing the improvement of the Social Order
By the avoidance of personal identification
With Suffering, a turning away to private sanity.

It is also specific to its time and place,
The uncorroded detail of vicinity.
These burghers and bystanders are our cousins,
But unlike us are encoded to accept
Adjacence as the only adjunct of Affinity.

The horror has to show itself: a grin
Is the keyboard of Sensation.
Technicians are consulting their circuit-boards –
Knives gripped between their teeth, the torturers
Are unwrapping the skin of Incarnation.

Gerard David, Bruges's Master Painter,
Enters a plea of Authenticity
Making redundant any further Judgement,
And yet by seeing simply what he sees,
Confronts Intelligence with its complicity.

The Violin's Obstinacy

It needs to return to this one note,
not a tune and not a key
but the sound of self it must depart from,
a journey lengthily to go
in a vein it knows will cripple it.
It would never have been born
if some fanatic touch of bow
and finger-board had not insisted –
it would have been the world
so timely unrevealed.
It would never have heard the E of deafness
or waded into the Rhine,
nor been required to watch
the conductor giving entries late.
So the note continues in its orbit
around its own elbow, playing musical chairs
with only one place to sit down,
its true death-bed. Like the trapped fly
in the window pane or the Abraham
of God's vindictiveness, it deploys
an endlessness of almost ending.

The Hungarian Producer Goes to Lunch

'Being Hungarian is not enough, is not enough,
there's so much else. Poor boys from Pecs
order their history from Maxims. Or swap with God,
a Raglan or a Ruskin. To be Hungarian
is to be German or English or American
since all the world will find recruits
in Budapest. An Hungarian is someone
who will enter a revolving door
ahead of you and come out behind you –
our sense of humour is renowned.
We are from Europe's epicentre yet
we worship Andy Hardy and the North-West Passage,
our actresses resemble Emma Hamilton –
they dance a little, sing a little, screw a little
and captivate the camera. They could start a war
if that weren't left to Generals. Our language
is like caterpillars dipped in ink,
and that is only its calligraphy:
it scans so well because it can't be spoken.
Isaiah was Hungarian and Elijah
and Jesus was en route to Budapest
when a passing donkey led him to Jerusalem.
We are the real Viennese. Not all of us
are Jewish, only those who've been baptised.
And what of me, you ask? I'm raising finance
for an epic film, 'The Magyar and the Mongol'.
My guests are late, a banker from Darmstadt,
a pecan-pie wholesaler from Milwaukee.
'Waiter, coquille St-Jacques and no Tokay,
just mineral water and today's *Le Monde*.'

River Quatrains

You never step in the same river twice
Although it looks just as it did before.
Only a perfect stillness will suffice
To keep Narcissus seeing what he saw.

Our prisoners we like to send upriver.
We load our troopships many miles downstream.
We are the true side of the Guadalquivír,
The other is enemies of the regime.

Our City Fathers' planning is polite.
The abattoir is on the edge of town.
Yet out of mind may not be out of sight;
Here on, the river runs a darker brown.

The Boat Race passes just beneath our windows,
We hear them cheering different shades of blue.
We don't get up and rearrange our clothes,
We're in a boat that's crewed by only two.

When Caesar led his troops across the Rubicon,
They thought: 'This guy's no Marius or Sulla,
He's Number One,' and shouted out his song,
'I am the Very Hungry Caterpillar'.

Alaric the Goth commanded that
The Busento change its course to hide his tomb;
In Cosenza now only the bureaucrat
Disposes of the dust which conquered Rome.

The River Jordan flows in semiquavers,
The Seine runs on past Seurat's tingling dots,
The dead on Ganges ghats burn round the bathers,
The Acheron parts Haves from the Have-Nots.

How doubly bright our minor river shines –
Its Bankside boulevards, boutiques and bars,
Its tax-loss growers of designer wines,
Container mud beneath electric stars.

See them gather by the river – Johannes
Der Taufer preaching that Messiah is near.
But those white sheets and that well-knotted harness?
How long, how long, before some God appear?

I'm on a river bank. I think I see
The farther side: a choice of nothingness
Or Paradise. My poems wait for me,
They look away, they threaten and they bless.